T0380185

A Guidebook for Young People Studying US Slave Songs

James Thomas *and* **Lorna Andrade**
Illustrated by **Virginia Stone**

To order additional copies of this book, contact:
Xlibris
844-714-8691
www.Xlibris.com
Orders@Xlibris.com

ISBN: Softcover   978-1-6698-0006-4
        Hardcover   978-1-6698-0007-1
        EBook   978-1-6698-0005-7

Library of Congress Control Number: 2021923488

Print information available on the last page.

Rev. date: 11/29/2021

Dedication

This work is dedicated to the unknown slaves who used musical styles from Africa to communicate, escape, and survive slavery. Many lives were lost pursuing freedom.

Table of Contents

Learning Objectives and Outcomes

By the end of studying this unit, the learner will understand the following:

- The African slaves were brilliant to use musical styles from Africa to communicate.

- The slaves were so very unhappy with slavery.

- The participants or learners will know how to decode the slave songs.

- The participants or learners will have many different ideas about slaves and slavery.

There may be other learnings, but we are sure that you will have quantitative results.

Codes—the Interpretation of Spirituals

The desperate need to communicate drove them to utilize characteristics common to their various cultures.

The call-and-response style was adopted from the African tradition of conveying history, current events, and directions between villages and telling stories in "Swing Low, Sweet Chariot."

Other common characteristics of spirituals can also be traced back to the African experience—for example, the predominance of minor keys and the layered tapestry of multiple rhythms and multiple texts.

Some spirituals are syncopated as in "Every Time I Feel the Spirit," and other spirituals develop slow, gradual chords as in "Nobody Knows the Trouble I've Seen."

Among the oldest spirituals are "Deep River" and "Roll, Jordan, Roll." They describe the crossing of the Atlantic.

The slaves wanted the listener to remember that "my home, Africa, is over Jordan."

what is a coffle?

To the surprise of many, most spirituals were not intended to be religious. The house slaves, maids, carriage drivers, cooks, and nursemaids accompanied their masters and mistresses to church to serve them.

They sat in the back and was fascinated by some of the exotic stories they heard from the Bible. They would return to the plantation and relate what they had heard. One such story, "Daniel in the Lion's Den," appears in "Climbing Up the Mountain": an angel of the Lord comes down and locks the hungry lion's jaws, and Daniel is spared.

The slaves quickly learned that the language of the church was safe and that by using Bible stories and images, they could disguise many messages and go undetected. The slaves became masters at the language of irony and the art of deception.

The masters and mistresses never knew that "Rockin' Jerusalem" celebrated the insurrection led by Nat Turner in 1831.

Many biblical characters and symbols reappear in numerous spirituals.

Chiefs

Here are some examples:

Jordan River. The Atlantic Ocean, which African captives crossed in the hole of slave ships.

Promised land, Hebden, heaven, campground, Zion, Beulah Land, and glory land. These can refer either to their homeland in Africa or freedom in US North.

Angels. Conductors/leaders from the Underground Railroad who would come to the plantations to lead slaves away to freedom.

Moses. This was Harriet Tubman's code name until it was discovered, then her code name was changed to Sweet Chariot.

Mary and Martha. These are believed to have been euphemisms injected into many spirituals, like "Rockin' Jerusalem," to avoid using real names.

God's children and the righteous. This is how the slaves referred to themselves.

Down yonder, winter, and Babylon. These are some ways that the slaves referred to slavery.

Some slaves acted as informers and told the masters what the other slaves were doing and saying.

In the spirituals, they are referred to as hypocrites, gamblers, sinners, and cowards.

Many spirituals express the hardships of daily life and the longing for release, either in the afterlife or in the North, as in "I Couldn't Hear Nobody Pray" and "Soon I Will Be Done."

Slaves who had to serve the masters and mistresses at the welcome table sang that "We're gonna sit at the welcome table one of these days." They dreamed of being reunited with lost kin in the song "In Bright Mansions Above."

With "Fare You Well," a slave who had been sold away took leave of his or her friends and kin, knowing that they would probably never meet again.

Deck on a Slave Ship
"Wasn't it a Wide River?"

A Guidebook for Young People Studying US Slave Songs

After the Civil War, slave songs that were created during slavery provided a rich body of work.

The Thirteenth Amendment to the US Constitution freed all the slaves following a long and bloody Civil War.

These secret sacred songs held different information for other slaves and slave masters.

The US Slave Song Project provides background, context, and interpretation for many of these songs and reveals the untold legacy and brilliance of these slaves.

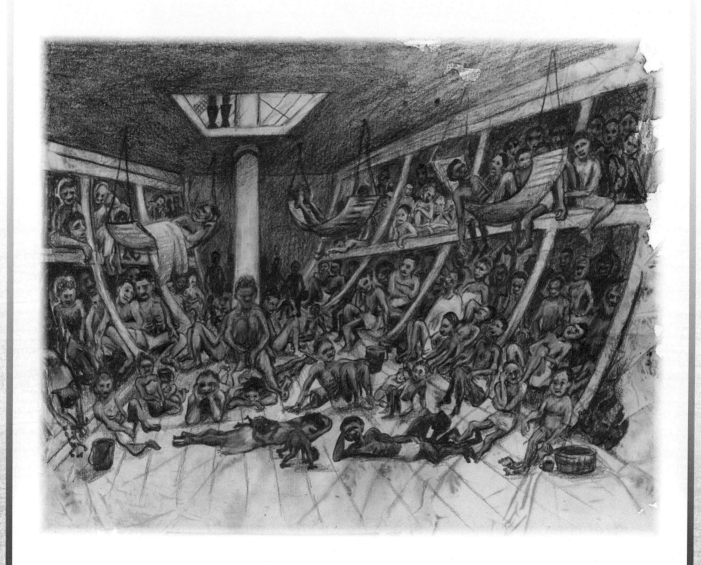

SLAVE SONGS:

1. Describe something (crossing the Atlantic)

Lyrics: Oh, Wasn't that a wide river, river of Jordan Lord

Wide river . . . there's one more river to cross.

2. Celebrate something–"Ain'ta That Good News"

Lyrics: I got a home up in a that Kingdom Ain'ta that good news.

3. Describe slavery–"I've Been Buked"

Lyrics: I've been buked and I've been scorned.

I've been talked about sure as you're born . . .

4. Inspire, give courage–"There's a Great Camp Meeting"

Lyrics: OH walk together children . . .

There's a Great Camp Meeting in the Promise Land.

5. Escape–"Wade in the Water"

Lyrics: Oh, wade in the water children

God's a gonna trouble the water.

The Following Questions Were Created Jointly by Young People and the US Slave Song Project

Why did slaves first sing these songs?

Children: Why do we sing spirituals [slave] songs?

Answer: To bring history alive, to increase understanding of our various cultures, to learn more about a challenging time in our mutual heritage. Also to acknowledge and validate the challenges each slave faced.

Slave songs were not composed like some other music; authentic spirituals in the US came into being between 1619, when the first group of slaves were brought to the American colonies, and in 1865, when the last slaves were freed.

Children: What was slavery?

Answer: Human beings were owned by other human beings.

There are descriptions of slavery found in ancient history. The Jews have been slaves in bondage to the Egyptians, Syrians, Babylonians, and Persians, onward to the time when the Africans were slaves to other Africans and European, Caribbean, and North and South American slave masters, as did many civilizations that built their economies around owning other human beings.

Life was challenging with inhumane conditions encountered on land and sea.

By sea, the slaves were packed one on top of another or side by side, chained at the feet and neck and hands; they laid in filth. If they became ill or died, they were just thrown overboard.

On land, the slaves were used for free labor, whipped, and salt or brine was thrown into their wounds for them to sustain more suffering. Slaves were boiled in hot oil, hanged in trees, or accused of any wrongdoing.

Slave women and children worked very long hours and had very little time to rest. Women and young girls were often attacked. Clothing was skimpy made from burlap, dirty sheep hide, and wild or domestic animals' hides. They lived in thin paper like shacks, no running water, dirt floors.

The women often gave birth on the cold floors in very unsanitary conditions.

Slaves were not permitted to talk with each other during the workday, and many came from various tribes that spoke different languages, so they utilized a common characteristic, music.

Institutions of slavery tried to deny its victims of their natural culture; they were expected to adopt the enslaved cultures.

African medicine was practiced, such as plants, roots, and tree barks, etc.

Rugs, mats, baskets, thatched roofs, and walking canes were modeled on African examples.

Religion performed multiple functions of explanation, predicting control, and communion of brother and sister slaves.

Many spirituals express the hardships of daily life and the longing for release.

"Didn't my Lord Deliver Daniel?"

Children: Is it illegal now to own another human being in the United States?

Answer: Yes, it is illegal to own someone in the US, although we see today in the world that human trafficking industry is operating in the US.

Children as young as three years old are caught and sold to work sewing clothes and other forms of labor.

" We're Gonna Sit a the Welcome Table "

Children: When did slavery end?

Answer: In 1865, in the United States of America, after more than 240 years of bondage, the slaves now freed did not create any more spirituals because there was no need to use codes.

Many former slaves became educated and learned to read and write.

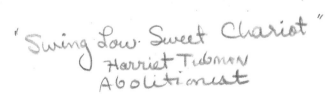

"Swing Low Sweet Chariot"
Harriet Tubman
Abolitionist

Children: Who were the abolitionists, and what did they do to help the slaves?

Answer: They were people who led the slaves to freedom territories. An example of this is Canada (Nova Scotia).

Children: Can you tell us a name of an Abolitionist?

Answer: Ms. Harriet Beecher Stowe, and she wrote the story of *Uncle Tom's Cabin*, in the year of 1850. She led many to safe places throughout the country.

Nat Turner - Abolitionist

Children: How did codes of songs get changed?

Answer: When a code was suspected to be determined by an informer or anyone working for the slave master, the slaves would change the code. For example, Harriet Tubman, whose code name was Moses, became Sweet CHARIOT, in the spiritual "Swing Low, Sweet Chariot," and the lyric "Comin' for to carry me home" was referenced to escape to freedom.

Servant Peter's Whipping Scars

Children: If these songs were not written, how do you know how to sing slave songs?

Answer: Many people learned them from family members who taught them to family members. Many codes have been lost. Many colleges that were created to educate former slaves documented slave songs and published them. Groups sprang up across the South to sing slave songs. The most successful was the Fisk University Jubilee Singers. The Jubilee Singers are credited with introducing spirituals to the world.

The US Slave Song Project attempts to sing slave songs as it is believed the slaves sang them!

Note: *No 12-part harmonies*

   No changing keys

   Just a high part and low part

Picking Cotton

Children: Did the slaves go to church?

Answer: Slaves would often accompany their slave masters to church to serve them. There were carriage drivers, cooks, and nursemaids etc. They observed how comfortable their masters were in church with the language of the church. These slaves, using music techniques from Africa, began to develop the spirituals using "church language," in as a means of communication.

Children: Were slaves considered stupid?

Answer: YES, slaves were considered stupid. They were not allowed to talk or learn to read or write; therefore, their songs were thought to be innocent.

Children: Do most people today have a good understanding about slavery?

Answer: NO, it is a distorted view in the eyes of many people, because few documents were written from the perspective of the slave. When we educate people about each spiritual, we gain a more accurate view and understanding of slavery. Little is known about each individual slave, but each spiritual describes events, survival, escapes, and other brief bits of slaves' life and beliefs. To many writers of the time, slavery was just a "leading financial asset."

RUNNING away

Children: What did an African look like before he was captured by slavers in Africa?

Answer: If a slave had been a warrior or chief of a tribe, he may have robes, spears, and wear a feathered headdress.

Children: Did the slave ships take slaves across the Atlantic?

Answer: YES, after 1806, when it was illegal to take slaves from Africa, slave ships stopped in the Islands to fix paperwork.

Children: Would you tell us a name of another country where the slaves were taken?

Answer: Brazil and many other countries, but more to Brazil than any other country.

"Follow the Drinking Gourd"

Children: Was London, England, involved in slave trade?

Answer: YES, ships were licensed and registered in transporting slaves; this was known as the Atlantic slave trade.

Children: When did Atlantic slave trade end?

Answer: In 1806, the British passed laws to stop the removal of people from Africa, thus making the Mid-Atlantic slave trade illegal.

an Easy Day

Children: What is the name of the great African port that slave trade took place in?

Answer: The name of the African port was Annamaboe.

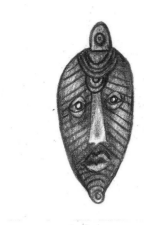

african medicine mask ceramic

congo medicine man

Oyo Yoruba medicine man

African medicine man mask c.1800-1900

Bearded medicine man mask Swahili

Children: Who ruled this place? And why was he a slave master?

Answer: He ruled a trading post by the Dutch on the West African Gold Coast. The [chief], a wealthy Ghanaian of the Fanti people, who was John Corrente, he was a known trader in gold and slaves.

He also sent a son, William Ansah Sessarakoo, to Europe to learn the ways of the European business to improve his trading prospects.

When his son was traveling with the captain of the ship, who was engaged to take his son to Europe, decided to sell him into slavery. That captain died, and his father discovered the treachery and refused to deal with the English traders until his son was released. To avoid diplomatic problems, the Royal African Company arranged for local merchants to pay for Sessarakoo to be freed.

Sessarakoo was taken to London, where he came under the protection of George Montagu-Dunk, 2nd Earl of Halifax, president of the Board of Trade. He was treated as a foreign prince, the "Prince of Annamaboe," and he became a celebrity. He also was baptized in London, England.

His portrait was painted in oils by Gabriel Mathias in 1749; his story was the inspiration for a poem by William Dodd, "The African Prince." His memoirs were published in 1750 as *The Royal African or Memoirs of the Young Prince of Annamaboe*. He later returned to Africa.

stop on the Underground Railroad

Children: Were there ever Negro masters that were good people by helping the slaves?

Answer: YES, they would purchase the slaves and set them free when they could.

Escaped Slave Looking though fence at Quilt for messages

Children: What was a group of slaves tied together called?

Answer: When the slaves were being transported in lineup, it was called a COFFLE. The slaves were bound at the neck side by side in a line of a dozen or more.

Log Cabin Quilt - You've Reached a Safe Place

Children: Did the slave children have to walk with a COFFLE?

Answer: YES, the children had chains at the neck and ankles too, and they had to walk hundreds of miles at a time, and often they would not survive the travel to the destination.

Bow Ties
Someone Will
Bring You Fresh
Clothes

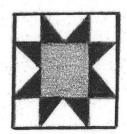

North Star
Use the North Star
To Get to Canada

Monkey Wrench
Get all the
supplies you need
For the journey

Flying Geese
Go North like
the migrating
Fall Geese

Children: What type of tools did the slaves use to work with in the fields or, if in Africa, in the gold mines?

Answer: Many tools were made and used, such as axes. Iron scales were used for weighing the gold.

"Sit Down Servant, Sit Down"

Children: Where is the Gold Coast in Africa?

Answer: The Gold Coast is Liberia, Gambia, Sierra Leone, and Cameroon.

Slaves Building the White House

Children: Did the African slaves replace indentured servants?

Answer: In the seventeenth century, the first servants were Immigrants from Irish, British, and German nationalities. When they became freed, they were replaced by African slaves, in which they took care of households and nursing of children.

Note: Indentured servitude was a working system when a person paid their passage to the new world with an indenturer for a certain number of years.

The British and Germans were among the first to be engaged into indentured servitude. Over time, they were replaced by Africans slaves.

Climbing Jacob's Ladder

Children: Did the slaves have doctors when they got sick?

Answer: YES, they had midwives for delivery of babies and healers for other health problems.

Children: Did the slaves have toothaches, and what happened to their teeth?

Answer: Teeth were treated by a healer that would pull out the bad tooth with a pliers-like tool.

SONGS #1

The Underground Railroad

1. "Follow the Drinking Gourd"

   When the sun comes back and the first quail calls, follow the drinking gourd. The old man is waiting for to carry you to freedom, follow the drinking gourd. Now the riverbank makes a mighty good road, follow the drinking gourd. Dead trees will show you the way. Now the river ends between two hill. There's another river on the other side. Follow the drinking gourd.

2. "Every Time I Feel the Spirit"

   Oh, every time the spirit moving in my heart, I will pray. Upon the mountain, my God spoke; out of his mouth came fire and smoke. There ain't but one train runs on this track, and it runs to heaven, and it runs right back. Oh, every time I feel the spirit moving in my heart, I will pray.

3. "Guide My Feet"

   Guide my feet, Lord, while I run this race. Guide my feet, Lord, while I run this race. Oh, guide my feet, Lord, while I run this race, for I don't want to run this race in vain. Hold my hand, Lord, while I run this race. For I don't want to run this race in vain.

4. "Keep Your Lamps Trimmed and Burning"

1. Keep your lamps trimmed and burning, keep your lamps trimmed and burning, keep your lamps trimmed and burning, for this race is almost run. Children, children, don't you get weary. Children, children, don't you get weary. Children, children, don't you get weary, for this race is almost run.

Colin Kaepernick Kneeling

SONGS #2

After death only

1. "There Is a Balm in Gilead"

   There is a balm in Gilead to make the wounded whole; there is a balm in Gilead to heal the sin-sick soul. Sometimes I feel discouraged and think my work's in vain, but then the Holy Spirit revives my soul again. There is a balm in Gilead to make the wounded whole; there is a balm in Gilead to heal the sin-sick soul.

2. "In Bright Mansions Above"

   Well, my mother's gone to glory, and I want to go there too. Yes, I want to live up yonder in bright mansions above. Well, my father's gone to glory, and I want to go there too. Yes, I want to live up yonder in bright mansions above. In bright mansions above, in bright mansions above. Yes, I want to live up Yonder, in bright mansions above.

3. "We're Gonna Sit at the Welcome Table"

   All kinds of people at the welcome table; all kinds of people at the welcome table one of these days. Hallelujah, all kinds of people at the welcome table. Gonna sit at the welcome table one of these days.

4. "You May Bury Me in the East"

   You may bury me in the east; you may bury me in the west, but I'll hear the trumpet in that morning. In that morning, my Lord, how I long to go just to hear the trumpet sound in that morning.

SONGS #3

Nat Turner insurrection songs

1. "Rockin' Jerusalem"

    Oh Mary, Oh Martha, Oh Mary rings them bells. I hear archangels a rocking Jerusalem! Hear archangels a ringing them bells. New Jerusalem, church a getting higher rocking Jerusalem, church a getting higher ring them bells.

2. "Were You There When They Crucified My Lord?"

    Were you there when they crucified my Lord? Oh, oh, sometimes it causes me to tremble, tremble. Were you there when they crucified my Lord?

3. "Witness"

    Who'll be a witness for my Lord? Who'll be a witness for my lord? My soul will be witness for my lord.

4. "Walk in Jerusalem"

    I want to be ready, I want to be ready, I want to be ready to walk in Jerusalem just like John. Oh John, Oh John, what do you say? That I'll be there on the coming day.

The First Memorial Day

SONGS #4

Religion

1. "Give Me That Old-Time Religion"

   Give me that old-time religion; it's good enough for me.

2. "My Soul's Been Anchored in the Lord"

   In the Lord, in the Lord, my soul's been anchored in the Lord. I'm born of God; I know I am. My soul's been anchored in the Lord. We shall walk through the valley in peace, we shall walk through the valley in peace, and if God himself shall be our leader, we shall walk through the valley in peace.

3. "Let Us Break Bread Together"

   Let us break bread together on our knees; let us break bread together on our knees. When I fall on my knees with my face to the rising sun, Oh Lord, have mercy on me.

By the founder of the Slave Song Project,
Mr. James "Jim" Thomas,
and MEMBER, Dr. Lorna Chambers-Andrade,
with illustrations by Virginia Stone

Bibliography

Aravamudan, Srinivas. *Tropicopolitans: Colonialism and Agency, 1688-1804*, 251. Dukes University Press, 1999.

Commission Bicentennial of United States Constitution, *The Constitution of United States and with Index Declaration of Independence*. 6th ed. Washington, DC, 1988. Eighteenth with Twenty-Seventh Amendment Ed., 1992. Amendment XIII, ratified December 6, 1865, p. 25, op. cit.

Kilbrideon, Dan. Audio: 59-12 (Discussion with an American scholar re: culture, history).

Louis, Gates Henry, Jr., ed. Introduction to *The Classic Slave Narratives*. New American Library, 1978.

Sparks, Randy J. *Where the Negroes Are Masters*. Harvard University Press, 2014, January 1, 2015.

–––. *Where the Negroes Are Masters*, pp. 14, 16, 46, 47, 48. Harvard University Press, November 18, 2013.

"The Process of Enslavement at Anamaboe, Movement of Slave Route," p. 131.

Wiencek, Henry. *An Imperfect God: George Washington, His Slaves, and the Creation of America*. 1st ed. New York: Farrar, Straus, and Giroux, 2003.

"Oral history is very difficult to interpret, and while a story may contain obvious errors, that does *not* mean it can be summarily dismissed," p. 12.

Wortman, Marc. "Secrets of American History," *True Colors* 45, no. 6 (Smithsonian, October 2014).

References

Allen, William Frances, Charles Pickard Ware, and Lucy Kim Garrison. 1867. *Slave Songs in the United States*. New York: A. Simpson & Co.

Boatner, Edward. 1973. *The Story of Spirituals*. Miami: Belwin Mills.

Dett, R. Nathaniel. 1927. *Religious Folk Songs of the Negro as Sung at Hampton Institute*. Hampton, VA: Hampton Institute.

Dixon, Crista. 1976. *Negro Spirituals: From Bible to Folksong*. Philadelphia: Fortress Press.

Epstein, Dena J. 1977. Sinful Tunes and Spirituals: Black Folk Music to Civil War. Chicago: University of Illinois Press.

Johnson, James Weldon, and J. Rosamond Johnson. (1923) 1969. *American Negro Spirituals*. New York: DaCapo Press. Reprint. New York: Viking Press.

James "Jim" Thomas, founder of US Slave Song Project Spirituals Choir

Jim Thomas was born in Humboldt, Tennessee, in 1939. He attended Fisk University in Nashville, Tennessee, where he studied history and government and earned a BA degree. While at Fisk, Jim was invited to sing with the world-renowned Fisk Jubilee Singers. Later, he sang with Robert Shaw Chorale in Atlanta, Georgia, and the Paul Hill Chorale at the John F. Kennedy Center for the Performing Arts in Washington, DC.

He founded and was the director of the Red Cross Festival Choir. They performed from 1976 to 1999.

He received awards in 2000, Red Cross President's Leadership Award, and 1999, American Red Cross National Diversity.

Jim held numerous leadership positions within the American Red Cross and special assignments for the IRCE, which included service at military installations in Vietnam and Germany and special assignments in Austria and Sweden for youth leadership. He was a team leader for MASH disaster assignment to Jordan and served as a team leader in Liberia and Malawi for friendship Africa. At NHQ in Washington, DC, he served as director of Program Development and Corporate Planning. Prior to early retirement, Jim spent his last seven years in the role of Corporate EEO, which included responsibility for minority initiatives. He has worked for and been affiliated with the Red Cross for sixty years. Jim has served on the Red Cross Board of Directors for Fredericksburg, Virginia, and Hyannis, Massachusetts.

The US Slave Song Project INC., a nonprofit 501(c)(3) organization, was founded by James E. Thomas in 2005 and is dedicated to educating the public about the history and interpretation of authentic US slave songs through presentations and performances. Jim is founder & President of The US Slave Song Project Inc.

From 2005 to 2007, Jim served as the cofounding director of the Martha's Vineyard Branch NAACP Spirituals Choir.

Lorna E. Chambers-Andrade, educator, RN, BSN, MEd, MBA, PhD

Lorna is a retired professor in professional nursing education, premedical and gerontology, and health administration and management.

She remains active with guest lectures and consulting at notable institutions of higher education and community health centers.

She sits on many boards and contributes as a public speaker, lobbyist, and author and workshop designer on issues ranging from strategies we can use for reducing violence in black communities to management of health-care facilities with a special focus on adult day-care facilities in rural areas, such as on Martha's Vineyard. Her master's thesis, "Opening Up an Adult Day Health-Care Facility in a Rural Setting," Cambridge College, August 1986, is used by many rural areas even today!

She is a member of numerous professional organizations, and she is listed in Who's Who in American Universities, Who's Who in Nursing, and Who's Who of Women Executives, and in the fourth edition of the International Biographical Center Cambridge, England, Men and Women of Distinction. She was a research fellow for the American Biographical Institute in 2006.

At the present, she continues to lobby for the rights of rural areas in regions to have access to local public higher education facilities. She continues to fundraise for scholarships.

She is a former vice president of Martha's Vineyard Local Chapter of the NAACP and presently a board member. She cofounded the Martha's Vineyard Spiritual Choir with Mr. James Thomas.

She is a member of the US Slave Song Project Spiritual Choir, which has a mission and vision to educate the masses on slavery with songs and history presentations.

She loves to sing and loves studying black history through lyrics and song, with a special interest on the evolution of slavery.

Virginia Fishburne Stone, Illustrator

Virginia has a master's degree in painting from Cranbrook Academy of Arts, Bloomfield Hills, Michigan, and a bachelor's degree in studio art from the University of North Carolina, Chapel Hill, North Carolina. She also studied figure drawing under a seminar for college teachers at New York University. In the Anthropology Department of NYU, she studied "African systems of thought" under T. Biederman. Virginia sings in Jim Thomas's US Slave Song Project Choir with Dr. Lorna Chambers-Andrade.

Printed in the United States
by Baker & Taylor Publisher Services